# BLACKBOARDS

ARTIST/POET COLLABORATION SERIES
NO. 1

saturnalia books

Tomaž Šalamun          Metka Krašovec

# Blackboards

Translated from the Slovenian
by Michael Biggins with the author

Introduction by John Yau

Saturnalia Books
7600 Cherokee Street
2nd Floor
Philadelphia, PA 19118
info @ www.saturnaliabooks.com

ISBN 0-9754990-0-9

Book Design by Saturnalia Books

Printing by Westcan Publishing Group, Canada.

Distributed by:
Small Press Distribution
1341 Seventh Street
Berkeley, CA 94710-1409
1-800-869-7553

Some of these poems have appeared in *The Seattle Review*, to whose editors the author wishes to express his gratitude. Grateful thanks as well to Civitella Ranieri in Umbria, where this book was written.

*Blackboards* was originally published in Slovenian as *Table* (Maribor: Litera, 2001)

Publication of this book has been made possible in part by a grant from the Ministry of Culture of the Republic of Slovenia, the Trubar Foundation, and IstraBenz, d. d.

Il sole baccia i belli e i brutti per consolargli.

—Italian proverb

# CONTENTS

All artwork is from "Trak" ("Scroll") by Metka Krašovec

# Introduction

Tomaž Šalamun is a prolific Slovenian poet whose work has been translated into many languages. The eight collections that have appeared in America have influenced many of our best younger poets. All but two of the eight books consist of selections from his many books and wide-ranging oeuvre. The exceptions are *Poker*, his first book, published by Ugly Duckling Press in 2003, and *A Ballad for Metka Krašovec*, which was published in Slovenia in the early 1980's, and appeared in its entirety in America in 2001. Full of intense sexual turmoil and moving reflections on his personal life, which, in part, were intensified by long periods of separation from his wife, family, friends, and country, *A Ballad for Metka Krašovec* was beautifully translated by Michael Biggins, who also translated the poems from this remarkable collaboration between Šalamun and Krašovec. *Blackboards* is the third complete collection of Šalamun's to appear in America. It was written in 1997, while the poet had a residency in Umbria, at the Civitella Ranieri.

Metka Krašovec is a well-known Slovenian artist who has exhibited throughout Europe. Influenced in her earlier work by Rilke, who is one of her favorite poets, Krašovec's more recent paintings are of women's faces and imaginary landscapes. Although she is a figurative artist, her work resists narrative, and the meaning is both opaque and open-ended. Krašovec depicts a private world in which the viewer sees hints as well as self-contained gestures and expressions. The world her figures occupy is abstract, sensual, and remote. The paintings included in this collection are all taken from one "trak", or "scroll", that Krašovec completed while in residency at the MacDowell Colony in 1999. The idea of painting on one continuous surface brings to mind the concept of writing over and over again on a "blackboard."

Šalamun and Krašovec define utterly mysterious worlds that parallel each other. In "My Wooden Benches," Šalamun writes:

The harvest was horrible among Count Ranieri's hounds.

But before you conclude that the poem is an autobiographical reminiscence about the author's time in Umbria, these are the poem's last two lines:

> I butcher sheep, and mother helps me. Ficino kisses
> my paws. If it smells of pine wood, it won't fade, Stubby!

At the beginning of "My Wooden Benches," a young schoolboy is speaking, but we do not know to whom: "Stubby? That's the nickname of a schoolmate whose/name is Zlatan." However, by the end of the poem you can't tell how many voices are speaking. Is one of Count Ranieri's hounds talking? Does Zlatan's unnamed friend have paws? The shifts and transformations happen so quickly and invisibly that you are convinced that you missed something, but you aren't sure what it might be.

Šalamun's poems pull you in, as well as seduce you into reading more closely and slowly. The language, particularly from line to line, keeps changing, like the world. "My Wooden Benches" evokes a world in which the relationship of the characters isn't spelled out, where the hierarchies governing the interactions in both nature and society are no longer present.

At once intimate and distant, Šalamun's poems remind me of portraits. But instead of giving the reader what, in painting, would be called a frontal view, a person speaking directly to us, a lyric "I", the poet offers us a profile, with his lines becoming distinct, tantalizing glimpses of an unstable world.

> . . . At the north, south
> left and right corners of all big cities
> there was a spittoon. Sometimes stations
> would replace it, but that didn't
> do any harm to speak of, except for frogs' mouths
> (from "Recollections of a Miner")

The voice isn't directly addressing the reader, the "I" doesn't presume that there is a shared space where revelation can be achieved. This isn't modesty on the poet's part; it is a refusal to believe that he speaks for others when he speaks. Being a poet doesn't mean that you are elevated, and experience the world from a higher vantage point than others. Šalamun writes neither confessional poems nor celebrates urban cacophony and the emptiness of the simulacra. His work does not depend upon a pre-established context. Rather, within their verbal boundaries, it is as self-contained and logical as certain paintings.

> A lion let out from its
> crate stirs up a
> tortilla and then stabs it.
>                 (from "Canova, Neighbor?")

Even in translation one becomes aware of Salamun's vastness. There are no obscure words in this little stanza, and the syntax is straightforward. And yet, the world it evokes shifts from word to word. What kind of lion is in the crate? Who let it out? Why "stirs?" Why "tortilla" How does it "stab?" What makes this inexplicable line even more powerful is that you can't picture it in your mind. Salamun doesn't write picturesque poetry. He's not trying to comfort you, let you feel at home.

Šalamun's rigorous resistance to the picturesque presents a formidable challenge to an artist who wishes to collaborate with him. It is also exactly the kind of project a strong artist might want to take on. Metka Krašovec is such an artist. Because it is impossible to see a scroll all at once, it becomes the equivalent of both a panoramic view and a book made up of discrete though seemingly connected scenes. And, as Krašovec fully understands, the format of a scroll can be used to both suggest and subvert narrative. Thus, on a formal level, Krašovec and Šalamun share a common ground: in the poems, each line or stanza can be self-contained, while in the scroll, which, for this book, has been divided into self-contained scenes, each page tells its own, open-ended story. Both poet and artist challenge narrative rather than reject it.

The luminous world Krašovec evokes through her delicate washes of watercolor is idyllic and austere. It is populated by nude figures seen in profile, butterflies, palm trees, a few rocks, water, and a pyramid. In this horizonless dreamscape many of the figures appear to be floating, as if the world they inhabit is made of both water and air. Aside from the figures, the one recurring image of a living presence is that of a butterfly, a symbol of both transformation and the soul. Often the scale of the butterfly is at odds with the figures. For one thing, it is too big, suggesting that it is between the figures and us. Another recurring disjuncture is between the figures and nature. A woman sits on a mushroom and plays the flute while a man clings to a plant, one arm outstretched toward her. Across an expanse one suspects they will never bridge, each courts the other.

This is a fairytale world, a place that is less sinister than Richard Dadd's and far less weird than Henry Darger's, but just as fully realized. Here, love, innocence, and longing never subside. The joining of the poems in *Blackboards* and the images in "Trak" makes perfect sense. For what Šalamun's melancholia and Krašovec's sense of longing set in motion is a dance of words and images, of words that evoke images we cannot picture, and images that define a world that cannot be contained in words.

—John Yau

# Palladium

**1**
I know nothing, don't ask much either.
Popcorn is buried with grenadiers.

**2**
I walked in at two.
Took ecstasy and moved like the light.
I stepped out at eleven thirty
into the sun, among transvestites.

**3**
I've eaten my elbows and sister.

**4**
What can you grab for dew
when there's a truce in the west?
Solstice and bread fall and thin out.

**5**
František heron is the gesture of gray.
Intelligence produces apples, pears and skyscrapers.

**6**
Seven puppy brothers.
And one mother cat.

**7**
A stool arguing with obsidian
will not shape a funeral for master Tales.

**8**
Quotation:
Thought is, in fact, the blood
around the beating heart. Bringhurst.
His arms dried out on purpose.

9
We've stung the subjugated.
Who are the birds that fly and fly?

10
We can whiten ourselves only with zinc.
And with grass and wood and a little ball.

11
Blueness is black and pealike and dim.
Larry Rivers didn't lose his composure.

12
O, empowering ones!
A plaintive body guides our leaves.

13
We too have endured
an enormous amount of harsh criticism.

14
Light tramples itself.
A tiny paw pries open just the padded ones' ears.

15
Wiping the dust from Cinderella's eye
is wet work.

16
A dull kernel,
white pearl in Coptic water,
we wash the flower in a tree.
Time rushes.

# Pumpkin

If I call to you from a pumpkin, I'm not calling out of daily
need. The darkness chirps. The pumpkin is aspirin. A stretched-
out face is everything. If you'll remember, while the torch

still burned I lost you on the steps, among the dogs.
Lupus in fabula? How does the torch burn? The wind
blows. It's all piled up for old ladies. Framed photos

on the piano are an anchorage. There's less space between
them than between tombstones. Under the blackness there's
white wood, beneath white wood are sacks that hiss into

the darkness. Have they been transformed into scrolls? Do they collide
with the rubber, hard? What causes the noise? Because somebody
had a hand in his mouth (two hands, two mouths)

making a braid which a silver wrapper slides down.
It doesn't go from there to some void. From there it always goes into a
straw basket. Che ne dici? I lean on the birds'

song. We've opened a window. Cobwebs brushed off
by themselves. What's more, we'll be able to bevel the river, trim
it with Amazons on plinths. Indians with their

kayaks squirt less than young folk with their
silver mouths. Cream your belly as you jump.
A train gets wrapped up in air like bread in white paper.

# What All I've Forgotten

I fidget on a chair and somehow doze off.
God broadens my ear. I snap. People on ships
really do toss hair, without getting haircuts.

We can see that it's tied up. But in fact people
don't leave the boat, don't get on it. Nobody
sings, nobody leaves for the army. The hugging is

an illusion. The stone of the pier is an open carton of honey.
Nuns stomped barefoot. The audience of the Hvar
Theater has left. A bee contains gray bronze.

Little pointed ears. In heaven there are handles and a matriarchy.
And you're gray, rotten and brilliant at once. The chart!
The chart! I eat infinity. I sniff the door.

Palm trees dance a rhumba. Too lightly. It's yellow
and stings. It's not under the sand, not under the oceans, not
anywhere. And yet it vomits and taps and sets and

draws anchorage. In summer it sets out to catch Zeno.
Mowing and tending fields. A pear is an idyllic
handful. We hunt for bell clappers in the fruit. Flour

donates wall hangings. White dumplings race through the lymph
of the glands. And a deer wrenches its knee, the deer's coat.
Pinakothek or paninothek, it really doesn't matter.

# The Otter

You are my menu, drift sand. I have no other
brother. To Mecca, among the logs, in a factory.
Flowers open up like umbrellas. The elements

lick each other and dance and box until three
in the morning. No. You haven't yet fallen into crinoline
pleasure. The taffeta is long. You drink water with it.

The bucket is insane. Not just lazy. How we shouted our
lungs out over the papers. In the tent right
alongside. We shifted and hid all

kinds of forks. Zeus had silver hair
and two handles on a topknot. He spent the time away
from Africa. Dermota was rowing. We wouldn't

let him. And we put on
a gray jacket first, then a red one, then
wings, then flashlights for our eyes, in case

we got lost in the Karst wetlands. They'd see us
with hooks. Who was singing? How are we
similar? I can slice your legs up to five

kilometers. Flavta lags behind. In Sudan a tiger
ate him while he was filling a tire. Just
blood stains were left on the spokes.

Aha! Aha! Aha!
The body isn't home.
It's gone to war,
to bring back rubble.

I'm having it flicked with pitch.

# Africa

Sometimes when I shine my shoes, the souls
start to squirt. You have to grow stubble.
The manuals close. The deluge subsides.

And the soul finds no expression at all, since
the current has stopped. Again!  Sometimes when I
shine my shoes, the souls start to squirt.

The shoe gleams, not the soul. There's no end
to these dead flies. They drop and the pump gives a whoop.
And if the sun's ring shoves into my rattle,

then all the more. I can raise my eyes.
I calm down when I'm furious. I'm prodded
and like a stalagmite. Benin speaks out of

the husks. His cheekbones have hardened. An otter
suits the window. Molasses is for the wound. For souls
converse with each other like electricity.

They endlessly leap at your fingers. And backgammon.
I can see a swamp in triangles. The man in the
hood knows what's at stake. To guard is to beg.

They're stuck together and half-erased. A pity
I've stopped them. They leak on my hoof. They leak
on my hoof. I'm alluring and lazy.

## At First He Tried To Drown Himself, Then He Emigrated

Peony, peony,
this is a yellow milk dish.
Overheated, Miša is still sleeping.
We pulled him out of the Mura.

Scout, kiss this bit of earth.
Rub your eyes in Australia.

The falls there run on milk.

# Olive Tree and Hair

A fly watches latently, I won't paint their faces.
The keys are pointed. I didn't defend the die
with a scythe. If there are no amounts, we don't cut into the flesh,

if we don't cut into the flesh, the abyss is gone. Prijatelj's
stable – gone. A block is a fist. The furrow
is famous and oily. In a sifter, in a white antenna,

in articulations, seen in a spy glass and mirrors.
Who breathes with flowers? Why is prayer an attachment?
I bury what I've ploughed, to avoid saying

goodbye. We dig the master a pear tree. Without
pressing on its seed. Prayer is
unambiguous repetition, till it sticks.

When it sticks, it whitewashes the aperture. It opposes
the ploughing. So I have the right. Lines are the
basis of style and prayer is a style. The way a

bird shits. The way fish fall. The way the earth
heals itself, because it ponders and ponders.
I stand just beneath the step where the

caterpillar for Mars isn't yet strengthened. Where the
river doesn't yet run. Where the flies are
giraffes and the giraffes are watershoots. Where all

around gold is distracted. Where Origenes
still lacks a throat. Where all that exists doesn't get stuck
on perception. Before dew strikes at the heart of God.

# To Sink

Son, the boot has really lain too long in the seal.
Wipe it off before the girl is awake.
My quinine. My rule. My zest. Moses.
Here, son, between moss and heather, mountains
and sky (there's an earwig in the underheaven) the spirit
senses and fills out the expanse as for dumplings.
Dew, butterfly, deer, bark. Amid the
bells. Beneath the corner. How can you set out a mousetrap
if you're tied up with ribbons (the papers promote your
immortal skin) and can't see a thing in the train?
Your head is on top of the luggage. A Macedonian customs official
is leaning, asleep. I've pasted several bands of
time together to enhance your saliva, prolong your
intrusion, your dance, your horror, and to light up the cave.

# Barbies

My hands are wet, just like ants'
little mits. Cellulae impressionae
humanae formae signatae out of
frozen flesh. Handbags have
ignited in the sulfur of the rails and taken the
raspberries. They grovel and all make
soft landings. It's a mixed pine forest there.
Of Vilnius, of Riga, of sport jackets and Judaea.
A mixed forest that swallows little girls' heads.
So that from third gear to second a mountain
gets sculpted. They're all on the square, they're leaning.
Glasses sit on the table, they're taking the cappuccinos
away. My brain empties out with a
spoon. Melancholy hemorrhages.

# Those and Those

Those and those little braids picked up for this place. It's winter
on the ice, and wet ears. They dry out. They don't
crack the skin beneath them as they adjust
to the cracks. There are eight windows on
each floor. The livestock is gray and far
out to pasture. The plane trees drop their leaves.
Not yet completely. I take off my tweed coat.
The village is in a deep freeze. My tweed
coat is the intellectual horizon of Rin Tin
Tin, of white bronchial tubes and the web of actions.
Factories that fell right and left into the
valley had shortened smokestacks among the
blackberries. The sailboat is at Barcolana.
Duino doesn't appear and makes a hole in our food.

# Rubber

It would have only been fair to soak Joan of Arc.
She smoldered on paper. A bone got a
mole, like on the moon, which you can only
cover with a bandaid. Frivolity is like a fine
cement windpipe. It fills your mouth like nicotine.
Then, when you close your eyes, you're a boa with the
world traveling inside it. Snakeskin or sandstorms on the
crust of the Gobi, both go through your hair.
Not through it, they compress it. For sunrise,
you have to cut through a membrane. If it's a sandstorm, you spit.
Saliva thins out the sand in the air. Swellings
form, then fall, and the sun shines
unhindered. Giro d'Italia or Tour de France,
the one crucified is always enamel and won't break.

# Fjords

A whale rests and flashes. A saga's columns
rumble from a white flowered meadow and go into
a trumpet, into foam. Will the whale's spout reach the
fjord's seventh shelf? Why did you have to put the
mattress there? It's too high for a giraffe's neck.
The gnome that is the motto will drink
all the goodness of the world and then spread it
like pollen, linking one floor to the other.
Once again, neighbors will call each other. Although they'll
be living like Indians in Puebla, and sharing
their towels. Just one will iron them. The toboggan is no longer
dangerous. And the whales that had disrupted layers
of air with their squeaking and water, that's where berries
will grow. Duba explains that Norwegians sell
their zucchini to Portugal in winter.

# The Drama As the Actor

Whoever takes it strolling won't last. The Stasi
arrest him. You're crafty, says the chief's son,
eating melons. No I'm not, the official says. I'm
here by the grace of God. If there's no seed there's no hair,
and without hair even a king can't fall. We look at
the coat. Everything from the pile put to good
use. Worms make humus in concrete vats.
The wagon is a trailer. If you put dirt in a balloon
full of helium, a drama will follow. God's muzzle will
tear up. The weather (so as not to have to define
itself) will hide. In any case, this slash is hilarious,
because in it you can re-knead the world and
try it again with a shape that's more round.

# JWV

Johann Weichard Valvasor, propped up on a pipe
in the clay, scratched himself against the lower left
edge of his carriage, so that even a servant
couldn't glimpse his elbow. He'd sold
everything. In shame he curled the door up.
The oak door had the qualities of a fan.
Everyone who stepped beneath this twisted book
ended up in hot molasses. That's why they called
him that. And why he was so sought after. For years
and years there was no higher-priced whore at the Waldorf
Astoria. He invented a new coat for hedgehogs. Johann
Weichard Valvasor (The Glory of
Carniola), and still the slice on his
pigeon's clay wheel snapped.

# Melancholia Fumosa

I strangled three kitty cats beneath
Niagara Falls. They bleated, even though they were
cats. I shoved one of them into a truck.
It struggled in its cloak. Another played
with an Easter egg. It stomped as we
drove. It had heels that were
really stilts, and had difficulty moving them
inside the car. The kitties are tuckered.
The railing doesn't help them. *Snap, snap,*
goes a stick when the stump catches fire. The wind
squashes their makeup and buries them. Quick ladies
carry everything away. The sky amid the clouds
scales when it knots up. Such was the presence
of three black cats at the market for a while.

# Vacatio, Ficino

A blasted, gaping oak of Saturn's,
it's the season for skin. Commotion
and Easter eggs peer out of the house, peasants exchange their
rails. Ho un sacco di lavoro. (Ad
secretiora et altiora contemplanda
conducit.) Rocco e i suoi fratelli is
Visconti's. Run a rake through bloodied
sheers. Put out the fire with a shovel,
so it doesn't escape through the vents.
An accordion shaking in silver. A tenth of a
kimono is a tenth of a violin. Silk gives way.
A tadpole floats in a tachometer's white shell.
The flower is in pieces. The handsome prince died of a hump.
Forza Bobby, forza Bobby, try to sleep!

# Narcisso Con Gli Occhi Glauchi

Emptiness hisses through turbines of flesh. What are
eyes like from mooing? An ox has legs like a
loom. Surveyors walk with barley in their

hair, as though they've tried and tried to
drop their reading. Would tongues be more comfortable
ripped out? On a shelf among crystals? In

cups unwiped by dust? Does the
British Museum even have enough space?
I trampled you in front of Hutter's apartments.

Your teacher caught sight of a deer. You crumbled
to a state of rest. Your hair fluttered, Branko,
even under your cap. And the bridge you observe from below,

on your back, after swimming. Can we then call
flour on its back a goldfinch? Resting in water
a pump? A turn of the light the commanding of people?

Only incest steams. It comes in waves from the
countryside. Pastries are wrapped in kitchen
napkins to stay moist. I am warm and pious.

# Pastries Hit the Floor

1

My shins hurt in silent papers, but otherwise,
no, would be my answer if asked whether
I had a happy childhood.

2

A sheep that gives human blood
is like a transparent Venetian stamp.
You won't find the one or the other before
the sunset of people.

3

Get up, Anita, brush your hair,
put on your makeup and go to work.

4

I've often joked until a
servant wiped my mouth.
Ten thousand people watch a hanging
because he clowns and salutes.
He came rushing in on stockback.
The stocks are pious and prodigal.

5

Power lies beyond the outstretched tongue of the sacred
colonies. Even on Crete, in the water, two feet
below the surface. Insects and peas have the best
view up God's legs. Oratorios
where you can walk on the surface. If
you kiss a single gesture, paint it, son.

6

I had a silk coat, now I don't.

7

A tooth has a duty, wetlands will follow.

# Windows of Umbria

The fruit tacks, it sails and tacks. Cabins. Of wet grass.
On the front steps a child. Singing. A lamb's heart
gushes blood. Are little hairs an ocean? Isn't an overhang

something that light creeps up on, that reduces the light into
a stalactite? A cluster of hands strikes a spark. A cupola yields
a shell. The pastures and flags and moss on the bark are

all made of clay. A skit is when you swim from the
early time to the late time. Snowball rolling
uphill, is the stone a diastole? The end

of a pillow portrays a kingdom. The voyage
of Camões. The gales, pitch and scurvy
of sailors. We sleep in the harbors. It splashes

the hull. A smokestack in Sintra is the window of a king. Haystacks
plunge into swords. One cubic millimeter
of apple is cardboard. A train races across

Tuscany, someone collects papers. The cases hold
brocade and spleen, and dawn reflects off
razors. Where's the legitimacy of an outstretched soul?

The strained ones get dyed. The stream has been dyed.
A laundress gets a white sheet that rests on the grass.
It bleaches on the stalks and the fabric holds up to the speed.

# My Wooden Benches

Stubby? That's the nickname of a schoolmate whose
name is Zlatan. I woke up on the third of Thermidore
last year. The wheat stalks all had fat heads, more than in

the Middle Ages. Boats float on streams of blood. The currents
are swollen as high as the bell towers. They've swallowed the boxes,
the white cardboard box that the head in Atelier 212

looked out through. Strudel is made out of raisins, cotton and the upper
crinkled layer of cardboard, where Russian villages smolder.
Pushkin pops a deer into his pot. The skaters

chase me up the river. The cosmos is frozen, whole, milky,
cratelike, and stretches out its plane trees like the petals
of a sunflower. The sulphur's persistence squeals light.

The harvest was horrible among Count Ranieri's hounds.
Eyes rose up from their bellies, separated and
rolled off, then joined again as snowballs. The snow

ball hurts. Palm trees grow up around it. The roots
gain color. So many images for the soul pass through them, Stubby!
I like the way you slick your hair. The way you copy out

the Coronation and how stuff bulges in your book bag. The white
one then rolls around our playground behind the wall, where they knocked
my teeth out. I also like the way you married

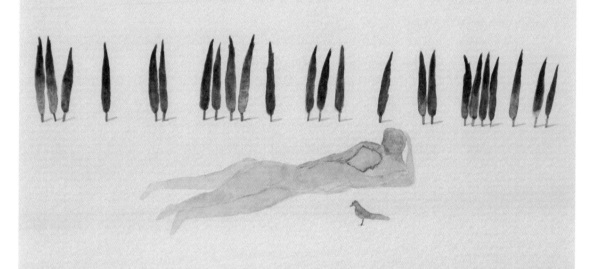

Ivette, and that we built eyes for her in the park. She raved
with them like a lump in an octopus. Relaxed,
we swam up to the edge. The edge of what? The edge of the

most horrible availability. I butcher sheep,
I butcher sheep, and mother helps me. Ficino kisses
my paws. If it smells of pine wood, it won't fade, Stubby!

# Park

My muscles are geometric. They're pierced with
pins like a mapa mundi. Generals rest,
generals sleep, they joke with their daughters.

Kutuzov was always blond. Now he's been turned
into curling papers. Whatever you set below exudes a scent.
And you feel violet mountains, violet ridges, violet everything,

a joint. Does the domino fit? Vanish among horsetails. Does
it clear up? And then I took a keeper of ice
cubes meant not to melt. Who will smell fragrant when

the water lilies have faded? Who will deepen the ditches
when the deer are all dead? There's no scent left
in ossuaries. They crumble flat out. A bone from the crypt in

Tomar, for a slingshot. There's a gleaming plate
on the asphalt in Fatima. Prayer has uprooted trees,
clothed mummies, insured them comprehensively.

You murmur when a bee takes more space. In two
enormous yellow cups stuck to each other
the races roar. Ledas cross paths. Chen Yi,

Chen Yi, it drips away. She guffaws, pragmatically
and technically. She runs the computer and calculates dew.
Yesterday we fell asleep in her embrace.

She provided us with chocolates. Do I subdue the clearing?
Draw extra fingers on the fringes of roots? Why
does sap run through everything, and through rusted ceramics

most of all? Gold's value drops. There have been
no such eruptions for thousands of years. *Frana!*
*Frana!* Watch out! An arch and a car rustle into the park.

# Gojmir Anton Kos

No resistance, so we're sad. Phedra
is full of glycerine. The cypress that should have
bailed the juice on Tauris fails.

I know the snail sees through mountains.
I know it's climbing. I see it
flashing toward the giants' jaws. The warm

belly of the cosmos is elastic.
Empty and protective. A scythe, a sickle,
a pin, machete. They're all the same. They

don't fulfill their functions. You apportion
death like cut timber, you shift it.
Do you remember? Gojmir Anton Kos,

before his death, the way the light hissed
in the icy candles on the Škofja Loka
roofs he painted? As great a man as that,

and he'd never even thought of such a thing.
While his wife washed his brush out
he shone, slumped over the light, and went out.

# Vivat

There isn't a feather shaft fast enough that I couldn't
disrupt it. Sugar was invented in cathedrals.
I'm single and handsome and covered with spots. The

hitches in my throat are cars. Soapstone
and a precipice were intended. Both are made
of clay. Both of them come from Odessa. The

tamburitza shattered on one of them, but he refused
to be scared. He drew his diaphragm out of
a quilt. At first there was nothing. At first there was a

swamp. Then they started freezing the fur on
drones. Crusteacea are abolished. Text falls out
the windows. Seawalls make the fish

shoot, and I get drenched in sweat on the back
of a camel when my bedouin begged. We're ready
for a silver platter. Wildness purges.

O, mortar! who've drawn a termite hill
and oracle. And gawked at bird
entrails, while at the courtyard's edge they're roasting

geese in pairs. Rome recovered. Job is a
brookman. Now that you've jabbed yourself on a handle,
that you've hunted for treasure and swallowed an archer.

Balm lurks among the cardinal sins and keeps quiet.
Lean over, little pocket. We're not accustomed to you.
We're handing you to the Obermeister to drag you out.

# Among the Hovels

Dobrila!
Last night I saw you with corn mush.
Could I ask you to explain that?
It was late.
I was afraid I wouldn't make it
and said I'd had a tooth pulled.

Dobrila!
Sign it. Say you're
Crustacea and the burglars' ringleader.
I'm going to rip off your mother's neck.
And during a pause, when the door-to-door salesman
breaks in and fixes his
gaze on the deer,
you'll beg on your knees.
You'll never, ever copy off another classmate.

# Hawthorn

I leaned my shoulder against a crickety grape bunch.
My tongue suddenly became white and catlike.
Geysirs itched and rattles oppressed them.

Besa me mucho, your perfect picture with Rin Tin
Tin. A vile chalvah (what's left of Dante)
swallows. And Mallarmé buried his little hands

so they would rustle throughout the Rhone. With a star
on our foreheads we spade with a pick. But that's where
the tractors wriggled loose. Caterpillars had

gummed up their tires, while moths
broke into the coat. Three elements are burning
gold. First fur, then a hoof, then

the felt on the keys. A white thread
gasps. Lips step into a circle. And coal and
peacocks and a shaven landscape for golf with all

the horrible disinformation about how they
demolished our oak door. Venice would be
standing without that. Pile dwellers would build it.

In the Doge's Palace they'd set fire to snakes. They'd
shake in their plumage as the flame licked
their coils  They carved out cities. They gave

their lives for the right gauge. And to this day at
auctions, whether run by hammer or by voice,
we uncover what in fact were footprints.

Dante was offered elegant canes
which he immediately turned into steps.
They drew him when the earth was churning. He cleaned

the hatches on his shoulders. The overcoats buzzed.
Little rings for the horses—they pressed them down like
pins and it was cold, but why

should it be when everything crackled and roiled
and flapped with napkins flocking off the tables.
All further functions dropped into a hawthorn.

# Quid Pro Quo

Perfect sentence, shake seed into my hail. A Tatar
seized a grasshopper. He rubs and rustles with his eyes.
He comes to a bell, starts to feel it, while the grasshopper

tickles his hair. Did he separate from
his horse when it slid? Did he use
Asia for his toboggan? Pedestrians have

their faces wrapped up in kerchiefs. Heights
grow up on the edges of shadows. Ninevehs travel through a
long pipe and then squirt out. Petty crooks

meet in the lift. Mercury in their hair
and on their loot. I'm round. Inky, so that
my lids widen. And when my neighbor downstairs

breast feeds her child on their deck,
the sun pants uphill. I told Iva.
Iva is preoccupied now with a slap.

It smarts. Cools down. A spider flings its
insect onto a metronome. And we're back to the
Tatar who saw his first stairway

and tried to lie down on it. Tucked away in
boxes and in niches, don't you think there are more
elements here than in a candy? History

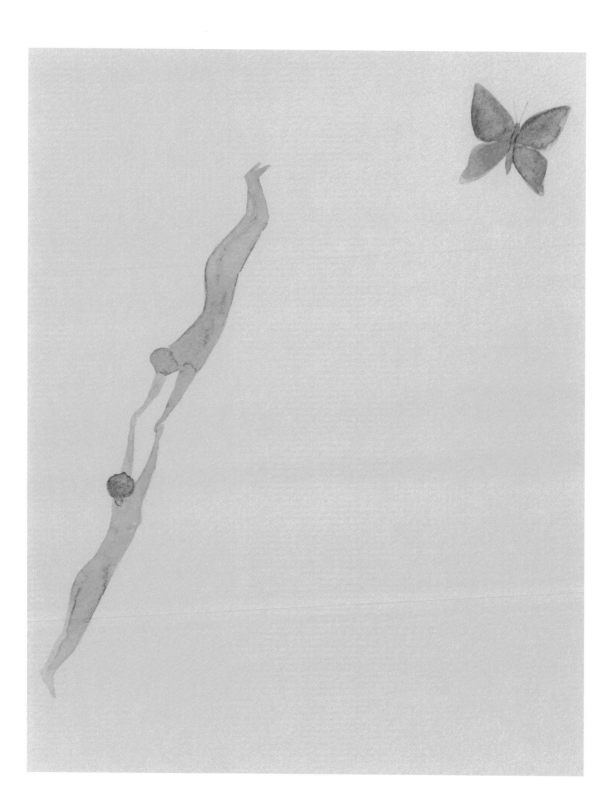

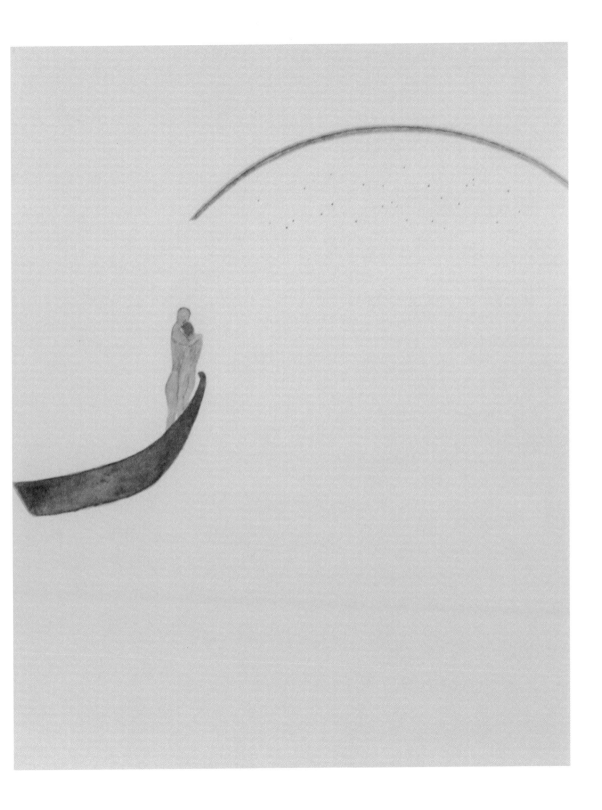

crouches. While you carve a cradle, while you slap a horse
(slap it like a cupboard) and you transport souls
with a mouse. Man is a traveler's bag. His eyelids

have smudged out the foreground. Lighters, forks, a
Nike jacket – I sucked them all out of bituminous coal. A wheelbarrow
stuck to it. Tennis, as long as the ball remains empty,

smells convenient. The edge of your racket
turns into a steamship. Set down the palazzo.
Stuff the rags and open up the silver spike.

# Gabrče

Wild animals that have imprinted their nostrils
on a quiver die. Their eyelids, eyebrows and
chaudeau burn. I see my face with the sun
in the water. A silent flower floats on the surface.
Lambs urinate. The pavement is stale and
contracted. Postmen wash, disturb the
water, rural postmen showing beads
of sweat. There's a bucket in the grass. The lazy sound
of a zinc-smeared boar is too far off,
though it flashes. Past the house, past the forest, it
rests in a beechnut and carries the midday in
its paws. The well is worn smooth, made of stone.
There are onions of churches. An insect runs along a
white wall. It runs into a corner I can't see.

# Auden

Savannah, Nebraska, the Capitol's
white columns. Flies zip by horizontally.
Gnats in their glinting haystacks
are invented. A white wall separates gnats
from flies.  It was built by Sušev Tone.
He had his lunch on a red roofing tile. Threw
the paper away. Then on that tile
he stacked seven more tiles and he
sealed the wall with mortar. Bees buzzed,
unglued from the animal kingdom.
Auden disliked France. He got annoyed
at countries where the lumberjacks
sang *Parigi Parigi* and waited for
horses and the exit where logs of hay would come out.

# Science

Struggle fits into kindness. A titmouse spills
on its leg. Lina writes an elegy for her dead
friend. A few fetishes shine. Slippers, a shawl,

long walks over the glinting sand. Here's where they
sat down. There's where they had lunch and
giggled. Then got up again. Wandered through the

glinting sand. Faces of sailors out of
*Moby Dick* and Nantucket in fog are included.
Frank read Chekhov in the bath back then

and now. How many times did they practically
have to carry him to the sixth floor when he'd wreck
himself and exercise. At his funeral Larry spoke about

his flesh, which kept pulsating two days past
the accident. History shapes itself into little spheres, it
forms like a new mutant animal species. First

your beak grows for millions of years, shakes and gets distorted
at a transition, and then pours into crystal. The orgasm
makes a boat. Storms, poles, wires over

the hops. If you don't distinguish between a dusty road
and stamps, does that mean we see better? Gorillas are
too gentle. They peal crusaders. You take a penknife,

peal your crusader and wrap his
skin around you like fragrant flower petals.
That gentleman in the sunglasses was about to

strangle me, but got scared. Or I just turned
his hair around. It curled like pistachio hair.
The sea is unimaginable. I water elements.

They paint and pinch. Then they stop pinching
and separate a bit and the sun really does
make a few little bubbles form on their skins

which they cool in the shade. I throw black coal
on the laudatio. I talked about food with a man who was
dying. About tastes that memory had turned to ash.

# Yo Yo Ma

Sin was driving at my jacket. I thought about
Pygmalion and swarming bees. If sugar gets your
gear shaft wet, then why do magic? Isn't it all

available here? The arm lifts. Like a pear branch,
antlers spread below and I understand Benn.
He was right to object: like, like, as though,

using these to sniff out dead ends. A forked
pear branch is no wing. Is that why we pick
berries? And what if invention is eternal,

spread out like a transparent fabric? And if you
go into a boat when they nail you into your coffin,
what matters is that someone tells you, calls you. That someone

says, "Isaac, you're dead." There's fog where a
mountain was. The sugar in the body escapes. Evaporates
like starlight. But you still feel.

Silent smoldering (no longer so strong, no longer
so strong, but it's nice the way everything
recedes) the cocoon gives way to gowns. Wine

is drunk. The numbers stop racing in one direction,
stop rolling across the floor or knowing what to do with
water. They're wrapped up in a sheet and stored away

to shine in oblivion. Everything changes,
comfort. We draw glory out of every
bit of youth. Those with slightly

smeary crusts (deer, doves, also little
pigs and cellists), Yo Yo Ma, see how he
gives. He shines in the master class. The sugar

just flies from his head, he can train in any
stable. The juice of life forces this abundance
of sound, laughter, love, of endless

joyful patience. Isaac, you're dead.
Good of you to tell me. Now I'll stop
bumping into furniture like some dead log.

# Stefanel Jacket

I stare at a shop window in Arezzo. My fingers rest on
the glass. A tunnel devours coffee, a triumphal arc is full
of tiny lights. A belltower rises from stone to seam, from
stone to seam, and then you spit with the birds from
Badia. In my slippers I covered a path to the *dotta e
grassa*. Where they had a mayor named Walter. A
wild boar lies in my storefront, shot by Maurizio. The peasants
divide into groups. I discovered it while it was sleeping.
Now it's broiling gilthead bream. Hardy meat shot through the sea.
I'm covered in basil. My campanile daydreams. I park
like an animal. I yank my catch up the stairs,
Metka. I break down the door and fling her on the couch so it hurts her,
it hurts her, it hurts her, till she groans like a deer. Deer
stand on the ice, watching the sunset, and sing.

# Trieste Mia

This apartment house doesn't know Roberto's hallway. Immaculate
*bingula bingula*. Step on the trampoline, jump on the
trampoline, according to your merits. The Italians are masses.
Grains open their husks. They illuminate their little
bellies, artificially. Nature waves its artificial
hands. It clones the gods new throats, so they have
new throats. You can feel them like two peas.
So who can carry them to the brains? The street-
cars' brakes give out and they speed into the valley. In the
valley there are piers. The whole streetcar pours onto the boards. I like
soaked wood. So that your soles rest on pitch that the
ocean washes. That's how I'm here: Fisherman's Wharf,
by streetcar on some sort of raft. I draw my
Frank in a pose like Larry did, after Géricault.

# A Poem for Atom Egoyan

You mention the harvest, when a
huge yellow combine first uses highly
complex maneuvers to make its way through the stand of trees?
Harvesting grain means chopping off branches.
The combine's tires are a
head taller than a grown-up and
twice as tall as Arshile.
He plays with a cat.
The cat wants to lie in his lap.
We haven't yet decided.
We don't yet know if we're going to take it.
Arshile is in his element.
He calls to Gordon the nicest of all.
Snow falls onto the level plains of Canada.
Memory straightens up like a victim.
Who is drinking the juice of Armenia?
When you walk, when you walk, will you
look back?

# Brad Gooch

The calf was walled into a new doorway so it wouldn't fall down.
They lifted it up by its neck like a cat and they walled it
in about ten centimeters above the floor. What I mean is,
its legs were ten centimeters above the floor. Then came a new
generation which had mastered the stenography of small animals
that shined like stones in rings, full of grace. Shined shoes or
shone. It began to crunch toward the heart. Stages were set using
pressure. I discovered Bunny Lang with bands. She kept
gnawing into my light, her hair, her exuberance,
her epic baths. But I never saw her.
I never really pictured her, since she died long ago.
Then comes Brad Gooch. Nice-looking guy, young, in a tie, with lively
eyes, lively speech, and now Slovenians have
tons of monogrammed neckties waving for them on the roof of the world.

# Recollections of a Miner

I could write tons and tons of comments about
chewing. How it grows wings, turns on
lights, throws its cap and gets all impatient

before it goes to the mine. Back in the days when
workers still flooded Trbovlje, we thought
highly of it. We'd come from our streets and

spit on the asphalt. At the north, south,
left and right corners of all big cities
there was a spittoon. Sometimes stallions

would replace it, but that didn't
do any harm to speak of, except for frogs' mouths.
We'd rip off frogs' mouths. We'd take sand

paper and start adjusting the side as early as winter.
Frog, sailboat and chandelier, we dressed
the piano in crinolines. The borders were crossable.

Otherwise the rivers would cover the horses' backs,
but since the horses could feel someone in the saddle,
they didn't drown, although they couldn't swim.

We'd sing all the way home when we returned with the
cloak. The nails on the boot soles were like
some factory producing shiny beads. You didn't

know if it was from plankton or fireflies.
Foxes ate up every box and plastic
bag along the forest trail. I

raised worms in concrete tubs to
get the humus. That's how I got
through socialism and attended Moriarty's funeral.

# As Early as the Tang Dynasty

Elijah goes flying off from Giotto
so that his wheels and horses
don't stick.

I remember a
bull that was there purely to
test whether our eaves

would hold. At stake
were a different nature and a quantity
of berries.

Grapes, however, are
off limits. Fish glint in their
basket.

And that's how the Island of
Vis and Haloze and the ninth century
all stick together.

A dense, drizzling
rain on a traveler who
waves.

# The Last Lighthouse Keeper

Check out, Moses.
Quit shining on the mountain.
Your blackboards are too

pointed,
unusable.
They're more like tetrahedrons than like breathing

baby elephants. Drawbridges come
into fashion,
moss for stuffing

pillows.
Where the light is mounted
now, there used to be pianists'

eyes, reporting on the
ships. The lighthouse keepers would stop
lunch when the waves were

too high. They'd move around on
rusty
struts,

and spread
a tarp in case someone fell through
the hoop.

# Canova, Neighbor

A lion let out from its
crate stirs up a
tortilla and then stabs it.

In the storm we lost
our boots and
hatchery.

Flashlights etched dew, but
only dew.
Some mountain men

waved their
flags.
While we rocked in

hammocks they smashed our
china.
And with a boiling bucket

I doused myself
staccato red.
We got Gerald

all worked up.
He babbled on about
the Three Graces.

# Varese

Tastes are made of tonic and pigs, so they're
mechanical, Russian, classic and stable.
What is Niemeyer next to Arcimboldo?
What is Arcimboldo next to Niemeyer?
If a camel can pass through a ring,
why shouldn't it pass through a hoop?
But it won't pass through a hoop.
It won't, it just won't, it just won't.
It gets stuck.
The Bedouins didn't make them tails
like Russian jets have.
Fish ponds of the empire,
I begged for a gunshot.

# Union Square

I was six years old when I ran through the Ptuj
Castle to grab a halberd. Why are you running,
Grandpa asked me. Katka hid behind a

door and faded behind a stove like some flower of
Gradnik's. Then I stuck all of that onto a stamp and
sent it around. That was the start of the domain

of stitched rags around the world, patches
riddled with Eurotunnels, and I didn't
lose a single stock, not even close, only

their value fell when I trusted
Steiner, such a gentleman, with such a good
background, in Cambridge, when he

explained that for the English the French were
rats, people like him just crippled rats.
Alas, no background can help

even the greatest corporate scions. They get
bloated, puffed-up brains, and at
long last Indians can dip their

arrows in their tunic and Ararat. Merku had
to collect the entire correspondence. Behind the
tile stove is where Dušan Fišer is exhibiting now.

They're taking admission. We drink beer.
And I attack him like a tank, to limber and
waken him. Metka thinks it's overdone.

# Giusterna

Stuffed ducks are a stitch.
They kill white rabbits.
White rabbits lack any foundation.
Their eyes continually
merge because they wear them on
soles. And whatever they
hit – gravel, grass, the
moss on stones submerged in a stream–
ouch! ouch! they cool their rattling eyes.
No! Bowlike. Pulpy! White! You can roll up
their lips endlessly, like a fax.
There's no pentola or memory left,
everything gets put in a treasure chest.
That, pandolo, dust, sparks,
a well-aimed blow,
a boat dock and sunset.
Salt to shine through your body.

# A Goalie and Why

No, language must push a hiker uphill.
The hiker has his own age, nationality and
head. He can't be a hiker a priori, draped in
little violet notebooks. His horizon can't
just vanish underground. Fantasy is one thing, siora,
a person of flesh and bones is another, wiping
his sweat, looking around. You can't just plane
the field, say Leda and the swan, leave him there
to freeze on steps where there are no steps. Where there's
a mountain, the wind blows and you have to feel responsible
for people. So come on down. You've climbed too far.
You have to call him till he comes down,
until he washes. Until he eats his
bunch of blueberries and peacefully falls asleep.

# It Sticks

I'm nailed.
Twice I was nailed
out of Russia's intravenous climate.
I carried a jewel box, built them and paid for it.
The Russian bear didn't work out.
It was fat.

Then I bet
my entire fortune, which hadn't
evaporated nearly as much as the Bologna
bigwigs think. They had fun. They crumbled me in
oil.

In huge centrifuges they stuck
green lettuce leaves to me like the sprout in
the fairy tale.
I behaved classically.
Put the box on my shoulder, left to a full moon
and–though wearing sandals–
did the hoeing myself.

Combining earth and olive branch myself.
What an oak.

# Maggio Selvaggio, High Above the Trail

I drew Fellini on a wall, an enormous fresco,
blocked him out,
filling his yellow grooves with
saltpeter.

The humor evaporates from wet
young girls, forever
fresh,
and that was my intention, too, when I
shined a flashlight in his eyes.

The newsstands are still there.
Snow is still produced with the turning of fine
metal.
Its own thinkers have stopped
patching the metaphysical pool.

Fellini shines in the sun.
Above all, he shines.

# Hugs

Let the explanations and the channels wait. Let
pride sink. *Vita, vita consumata est.*
How much gasoline accumulated. Lines on

the sides of husks, through the mountains, the isohips, between
mind and mind (on the lines we use for
drying laundry), what will Atom Egoyan do

now, when he goes? Arsinée, Arshile, I don't picture
you on those lines. Tickle! Tickle! Avedis Issahakyan,
Hagop Oshagan, Krikor Beledyan, do you know

how the tribe emerged, what kind of crystal it got?
Gérard, boy, they've tricked you, limos go to the
starving, the frozen and hungry of the third

world. Are you still going to block the street? You've forgotten
the movies where you resemble Andraž. Danton,
your near-crust, back then, back then, if only you'd

combed, sat down, rung, whatever. Now you're
a fat man. Fat men are inconvenient. Your melancholy has been
blotted up. With Atom everything burns. The way he listens,

or struggles with myths. Armenia, Eurydice,
don't burn him up. Don't turn him into a pillar of salt.
Let the love shuck itself slowly, like drops.

# The Sunflower Above the Gates of Hell

The bellows that wash soft cotton resemble a spider.
We empty everything into our handbags, from the shelves to the hungry.
The sadness of heavy-laden witnesses, fish mouths just
one inch away from air which is at least as thick
as a shoe sole. We clean ourselves. Our gnomes
strain us off. We are a fully conductive
ceramic. An invention of the craziest
lacquers. Our scent is decorative. We've been invented
to point to a bruise, a slurp, a whirlpool. Even a
rung on a wheatfield, it seems. I am fruit
of the sun. A shadow and a kamikaze of matter. The burnt
offering of paupers. My bones give off scent in warehouses,
are watered like Walter De Maria's Earth.
The watchman is frightened. He scarcely recognizes me.

# Pharaoh's Guardians, Mark Levine

How did you chase the flies off my sand?
Even the changes of linen are quicker.
The glue I used to stick a trunk
on an elephant (tape? a bomb?), don't you think
that your tracks are becoming too
simple-minded? Look at Mark, there's jade
in his green gaze, he never gets
in a truck alone, from outside he gauges its density,
age, blackness, traffic, even on streets
where the sun is bright. The sun's brightness, emergence of
blades. He uses wet telephone
lines. I manage to roll up just two blocks
of granite. The eye of God simmers him in soup
till he germinates and can take up his posts.

# Ralph

I'm put together like a huge leaden
vase, out of majolica and butter at once.
I keep watch over the Drava Valley. I imagined it
and made it deeper. My eyelids grow heavy.
They grab at the eyelashes, too. Eyelids, eyelashes and
raftsmen – plop! plop! To the left there's a castrum.
Why on the left, why such a stupid idea,
why not where Canetti and Ralph
Angel come from. Women go crazy and so do soldiers. They
climb up vines onto balconies themselves and rip off
the tendrils. All three of us Sephardim use
white makeup. Our eyes have been whisked, and most
closely resemble the fuzzy, dreamy
gaze of sad Etruscan dogs.

# Edoardo's Pathetic Carelessness

I opened up huge soles and out of them poured
water. Thunder and lightning are my brothers, we argue.
Edoardo forgot his shoes beneath the bed, he put on

sandals and drove off. Paola didn't find them and
swept only after I shoved the bed aside,
bent down, found them there, brown and with

socks in them. You'd do better to forget your feet, I write
and wrap the shoes up in a bundle to give Mariuccia,
who packs them better. Who takes them to the post office.

She can bring me the receipt later, here's some cash.
I lean on a white stucco wall and
do exercises for my back. Soon I'll be

well and able to wander the world
again, straight as a candle. I'll drive to
Denver. The place where Kerouac died.

The mouth of heaven yawned. They've set out prostitutes.
At the border he saw God in the clouds. The sultriness is black.
Last night Artaud dug me a precipice.

# Todi

I was sitting on the steps and eating grapes.
Cats chased each other dirtily around the fig trees.
It was time, the lesson was starting, but we were still

lazy, sleepy and bloodied. Last time I
climbed these steps it was night.
After a sweltering day the flowers were blooming.

At night? Sure. And it was pouring buckets,
fetid water attacking the drought. And I
endlessly sketched and sketched and sketched, and

life went by with me standing
under eaves. For Easter the sky laid
glimmering gilt spheres, which then

accumulated like gray frog roe. From one
corner to the next there was no depth. In the middle of
Italy I was reading Djilas. The rowers were

quick and malicious. When they'd get the
gauzes on their blisters changed, they'd give a whoop. And the fish
would shove globes upstream with their snouts, dive

under and stir up the plankton. In August you
want strength. But in fact a long, green
cord wraps itself around your belly between chapters.

# Beastlike Fury and a Minuet

A mutant stares at the sun. Oafish, beastlike
fury spent the night in a ravine and eased up on
its traps. It wrestled with paratroopers. As

Gradnik approached from the ridge to the left, we
waved to him. I'd like to make a hurricane.
So that the subcontinent's legs gum up and

start working like a single leg. So that a
cricket could have a life jacket just like a
bug or a swollen chocolate, which has layers and

layers of luminous courts. A separate stall for the horses!
Where the mother horse peacefully purrs to her golden
foals while audiences are held at the court and

the masters wash up. Crickets have never been
cooked in the same kind of pots as Farinata. They have
wandered wet into herbariums, that's true, but they

did all dry nicely over the years. I went down
Kafka's throat. I didn't recommend him. I said,
here, take this, and he spat into my palms. The empire

that combusted afterward paid me for it.
A thousand locusts swarmed at the ceramic parts of the
stove. The brocade on the night watchmen's coats has been written out.

# Tiger

We're not going to rock you.
We're going to eat you.
We'll pour off the shine from the skewer.

An eye glows at the Buna's source.
The scouts are quiet. The penicillin is quiet.
Whatever comes doesn't veer off.

The road from too much food needs powder snow, needs
powder snow, how many tires the air cuts through.
They've shaken quinine on the moss and now it's

boiling, now it's boiling. You don't even
know what quinine looks like, and still you
use it. If you ask me everyone boils

in Africa. If they think up a dolphin in the
Sahara, it doesn't pay off. What pays off are
tigers and lions and white rags

which they use only in places
where there are benches. Is it worth it
to accept an object like that in the jungle?

Or even in Cameroon,
with its trade in grain. The bags
empty out. A rucksack fills on the

steps. You break some off, I break some off,
the bread is holy. Grappa seeks its
truffles. They'll steal our Tiger.

The mailman carried off our little puppy,
made him famous, and then came the
hunters, demanding the other three

so they could raise them. How
could we not be glad, since
we'd wished for them. Now we regret it.

Tiger has no brothers, no sisters.
Now we've even bought him a red
neckerchief so they won't steal him.

# Flour

Distinguish! Drama from Ostrogoth, pine
tree from stubble. Distinguish violet clouds and
clawlike factories. Rut
fast, as fast as you can, the poplars will
tap you dry in any case. They grow faster than Mussolini
blinks. Their leaves are orchids.
Distinguish value. Don't buy Comit and
Italgas stocks together,
they boil over in your vats, in your
swollen nights they try to
sail to shore. All my
lives have been constructive. I've studied
my devastated cities. I even petted
Attila's cat when his coat burned up.

# Heated Passions

Let's look:
At what split apart.
At what opened bread.
Two loaves of bread, white hands.
Burnt fields, little hands.
At what touches the dream.
Words stick.
You'll forget what you dance off.
What you dance you give away.
Inside here is a castle.
The dampness is practical.
Access is in the apertures.
They break loose from iron and lead, hoops.
A farewell terminates the slide.
Soldiers whoosh out of a village.
The nucleus has been filled, is protected, has a white skin.
Power chews at everything.
What we've carved out will fall.

*Civitella Ranieri, summer 1997*

Also Available from saturnalia books:

*The Babies* by Sabrina Orah Mark
WINNER OF THE SATURNALIA BOOKS POETRY PRIZE 2004

*Apprehend* by Elizabeth Robinson
*Father of Noise* by Anthony McCann
*Nota* by Martin Corless-Smith
*The Red Bird* by Joyelle McSweeney
*Can You Relax in My House* by Michael Earl Craig

*Blackboards* is the first of a series of collaborations between artists and poets for saturnalia books.

*Blackboards* was printed using the fonts Tiffany and Stone Serif.

www.saturnaliabooks.com